D0757671

A BLUE BANNER BIOGRAPHY

Avril Lavigne

By Kathleen Tracy

Mitchell Lane
PUBLISHERS

P.O. Box 196
Hockessin, Delaware 19707
Visit us on the web: www.mitchelllane.com
Comments? email us: mitchelllane@mitchelllane.com

Printing 1   2   3   4   5   6   7   8   9

Blue Banner Biographies

Library of Congress Cataloging-in-Publication Data
Tracy, Kathleen
     Avril Lavigne / Kathleen Tracy
        p. cm. - (A Blue banner biography)
     Includes bibliographical references (p.), discography (p.), and index.
     ISBN 1-58415-314-8
        1. Lavigne, Avril, 1965 - Juvenile literature. 2. Singers - Canada - Biography - Juvenile
Literature. I. Title II. Series.
ML3930.L25T73 2004
782. 42166'092--dc22
                                                     2004009173

ABOUT THE AUTHOR: Kathleen Tracy has been a journalist for over twenty years. Her writing has been featured in magazines including The Toronto Star's "Star Week", *A&E Biography* magazine, *KidScreen* and *TV Times.* She is also the author of numerous biographies including "The Boy Who Would be King" (Dutton), "Jerry Seinfeld" - The Entire Domain" (Carol Publishing), "Don Imus - America's Cowboy" (Carroll & Graf), "Mariano Guadalupe Vallejo," and "William Hewlett: Pioneer of the Computer Age," both for Mitchell Lane. She recently completed "God's Will?" for Sourcebooks.

PHOTO CREDITS: Cover: Jim Cooper/AP Photo; p. 4 Evan Agostini/Getty Images; p. 7 Kevin Winter/Getty Images; p. 12 Dave Hogan/Getty Images; p. 16 Jason Nelson/Getty Images; p. 22 Jim Cooper/AP Photo; p. 27 Gregg DeGuire/WireImage.com.

ACKNOWLEDGMENTS: The following story has been thoroughly researched, and to the best of our knowledge, represents a true story. While every possible effort has been made to ensure accuracy, the publisher will not assume liability for damages caused by inaccuracies in the data, and makes no warranty on the accuracy of the information contained herein. This story has not been authorized nor endorsed by Avril Lavigne.

CONTENTS

Although she would become famous as a hard-charging rock and roll singer and musician, Avril Lavigne's first break was singing a duet with country music superstar Shania Twain. She got the opportunity after winning a local radio contest.

A Dream Duet

*I*t was literally the opportunity of a lifetime. In 1999, Shania Twain was the queen of country music and one of Canada's most popular performers. To help promote her upcoming performance in Ottawa, the capital of Canada, Shania agreed to participate in a radio contest. The grand prize winner would be flown to Ottawa to attend the concert. Even better, the winner would be invited to sing a duet with Shania during the concert.

Not surprisingly, thousands of people entered the contest. The winner was a 14-year-old girl from the small town of Napanee named Avril Lavigne.

The concert was held at Ottawa's huge Corel Centre in front of a sold-out crowd of 20,000 excited fans. The audience included a group of Avril's family and friends who had traveled to watch her share the stage with

Shania. Most people, regardless of their age, would have been nervous. Not Avril. "As soon as I walked out in front of 20,000 people, I'd never smiled so much in my life—it was like perma-smile," Avril later recalled in an interview with Chris Willman of *Entertainment Weekly*. "And I thought, 'This is what I'm going to do with my life, walk out on stage, have my own band, and be doing my own concert with my own songs.' I'm serious—this was meant to happen to me."

> *Avril displayed confidence and a lack of inhibition that would make her a pop icon.*

Displaying the same confidence and lack of inhibition that would soon help make her a pop icon, Avril held her own with Twain. When Shania told the audience that Avril was from "Nepean," the teenager politely corrected her. Then she proceeded to sing "What Made You Say That?" with Shania.

When the song ended, the crowd erupted into cheers. "It was the biggest rush of my life," Avril told the *Sunday Mirror*. "I was the happiest person in the world."

She went on to tell Shania and the audience that one day she, too, was going to be a famous singer.

A couple of years later, Shania appeared on the Much Music cable channel, a Canadian version of MTV. The host surprised her by playing a pre-recorded question from a mystery fan: "Do you remember me? I sang in Ottawa at the Corel Centre with you. We sang "What Made You Say That?"

Avril knew from the time she was ten years old that she wanted to be a famous singer and was determined to do whatever it took to make that dream come true, including teaching herself to play the guitar.

A stunned Shania did remember. She had a confession to make. For the past two years, her family and friends had been telling her that pop sensation Avril Lavigne was the same young girl who had sung with her at the Corel Centre. Shania hadn't believed them. She didn't recognize the punked-out pop star as the young girl she had met from Napanee. Back then, Avril had been completely different. She had short fuzzy hair and a preference for singing country songs. Once Shania realized that her friends had been right, she promised to send Avril a video copy of their duet.

The duet with Shania Twain marked a turning point in Avril's life.

It was a fitting gesture. The duet had marked a turning point in Avril's life. When she returned to Napanee after her trip to Ottawa, she dedicated herself to doing whatever it took to become a star performer. She immediately picked up a guitar and started teaching herself to play. In a remarkably short time, her promise to be a famous singer would be fulfilled beyond her wildest dreams.

A Small Town Girl

*A*vril Lavigne was born in Napanee, Ontario, on September 27, 1984. Her parents are John and Judy Lavigne. Her dad works as a telephone technician, while her mother is a homemaker. With only 5,000 residents, Napanee is the kind of place where everyone knows each other.

From the time she was just a toddler, Avril became known as the kid who loved to sing and perform. The middle of three children—she has an older brother Matthew and a younger sister Michelle—Avril always wanted to be the center of attention. She told VH1.com, "I remember when I was really young, standing on my bed like it was a stage, singing at the top of my lungs and visualizing thousands of people surrounding me."

Avril's deeply religious parents supported their daughter's passion for music. Her mom Judy sensed that her daughter had a special gift and told writer Ann Marie McQueen of the *Ottawa Sun*, "I knew I had to get her singing." Judy convinced her church to organize a children's choir. It wasn't long before Avril was campaigning to perform more solos. Her persistence paid off when she was picked to sing a solo at a Christmas service at the age of 10. Dressed in all white and wearing a tinsel halo, Avril played an angel and sang "Near to the Heart of God."

Although she was young when she started singing, Avril's ability impressed the audience.

Even though she was so young, Avril's ability impressed the audience. Soon she was getting requests to sing at various events in Napanee and the surrounding area. Avril performed wherever and whenever she could, from appearing in school musicals and at country fairs to entering local talent shows and singing contests. Everywhere she went, the audiences loved her.

"When I was little, people used to always say to me, 'You're going to be famous one day,'" she would later recall to Mike Ross of the *Edmonton Sun*. "I don't know, I kind of always thought I would. Not in a cocky way or anything. Everyone knew me as the singer girl around town. I believed in myself. I have like a huge dream. That's all I ever thought about and I think that I wanted it so much and that's why it happened."

Avril attended Westdale Public School but transferred to a private Christian school after fourth grade because some of her classmates bullied her. She loved her new school, Cornerstone Christian Academy, and quickly made friends.

One of those friends was Chelsea Doreen. Chelsea told Ann Marie McQueen that Avril was "always funny and always doing crazy stuff." She also remembered the day "we were going down the stairs and she hands me a piece of paper and she says 'That is going to be worth something someday.' She knew."

Avril was a tomboy and spent time dirt-biking and going on camping and canoeing trips with her family.

An admitted tomboy, Avril was a talented athlete who set a triple jump record at the 1998 Christian Schools and Homeschoolers annual track and field competition. She also spent time dirt-biking and going on camping and canoeing trips with her family. She told *Entertainment Weekly* that she tried every sport her older brother Matthew was interested in. "If he played hockey, I had to play hockey. He played baseball, I wanted to," she said. "I'm just not a girlie

Avril is known for her "skater-punk" style. But while growing up in Napanee, she had looked very different. Her friends remember her wearing conservative clothes.

girl. You probably won't find me walking around in a dress and high heels for a few years."

But singing remained Avril's overriding passion. When she graduated from Cornerstone, she was honored with the school's Marie Cowling Memorial Award for her musical ability.

Avril attended high school at the Napanee District Secondary School. Unlike her Christian grade school where everybody seemed to know and get along with everyone else, the high school was segregated into cliques, or groups, such as jocks, Goths and skaters. Typically, she ended up becoming friends with the skaters.

She was convinced it was a matter of time before her dream of becoming a professional singer came true.

Although she enjoyed her friends, Avril admitted to *Exclusive Magazine*, "I got treated differently by different people. I was a skater and there were preps who looked down on you because you wore baggy clothes. But it was OK."

When she wasn't out skateboarding with her friends, Avril continued to perform. She became convinced it was just a matter of time before she met the person who would help her make her dream of being a professional performer come true.

Looking for Opportunities

Not only did Avril love singing but she also earned a reputation as a talented actress when she appeared in plays at Cornerstone. That background came in handy when director Tim Picotte cast Avril as Sally in a 1996 production of *You're a Good Man Charlie Brown* at the nearby Selby Community Theatre. He recalled how Avril, then just 12, spent hours perfecting a hairstyle for her character. "She imitated it perfectly, I swear, her hair was half the size of her," he told Ann Marie McQueen. "She did it up like that herself, every night."

Two years later Picotte cast her as a rebellious teenager in *Godspell*. Ironically, when he suggested she wear an outrageous costume, Avril resisted. At that time she didn't feel comfortable wearing punk clothes. "Obviously that has changed within the past few years."

The thing he remembered most about Avril was her ambition. "I think she probably told us the first week she was going to be a star," he said.

Not long afterward, Avril began feeling discouraged. In her interview with Ann Marie McQueen, Judy Lavigne said that Avril was getting bored with singing the same gospel and country songs all the time. She was tired of performing in front of small, unresponsive crowds. What happened next wasn't surprising.

Avril was bored with singing the same gospel and country songs all the time.

"A lot of people wanted her to sing and she didn't want to," Judy said. Her mother would have to make excuses why Avril suddenly didn't want to sing. That wasn't all. Avril also stopped taking piano lessons and resisted attempts by her dad to teach her to play the guitar.

Things started to turn around for Avril emotionally when she performed at the Quinte Spirit Festival in 1998. The festival's founder was Stephen Medd, a friend of Avril's dad. On his website, which includes many pictures of Avril at the age of 14, Medd explains that the festival was meant "to inspire musical and artistic creativity in the Napanee-Quinte region and to celebrate the region's natural beauty."

Medd, a singer and a composer, also decided to record a CD to raise prize money for a songwriting contest. He wrote a song especially for Avril to record, a country-gospel song called "Touch the Sky."

As Avril got older, her taste in music began to change. Instead of enjoying country songs she started to branch out into other kinds of music. But one thing that always stayed the same was her joy of performing in front of an audience.

It was Avril's first time in a recording studio, but she felt right at home. It helped that her dad was on hand, playing bass guitar on the track.

"I realized that after one take this 14-year-old gal had a special talent and a great ability to interpret the new song I had written for her," Medd says on the website. Avril also sang two additional songs on Medd's second CD, *My Window to You*.

Not long after she finished recording the songs, Avril won the radio station contest. Medd and others from the Quinte Spirit Festival were among those who accompanied her to Ottawa to see her perform with Shania Twain. The experience of performing in front of so many people energized Avril and re-ignited her ambition. When she returned from the trip, she decided to teach herself the guitar and spent hours learning chords.

> *Performing in front of so many people energized Avril and re-ignited her ambition.*

The Quinte Spirit CD was released in the fall of 1999. That Christmas, Medd threw a party at Chapters Bookstore in Kingston, a city not far from Napanee. On his website, Medd recalls, "While a few of us sang a few songs to promote the CD which was being sold there, there was a man videotaping Avril."

The man watching Avril singing karaoke songs was Cliff Fabri, who would soon begin guiding her career.

Cliff Fabri became Avril's manager and soon began guiding her career.

"When I first saw her, I liked her voice, and obviously the looks," Fabri would later recall to *Entertainment Weekly.* "But it was the attitude. I was like, yeah! I loved the toughness."

Even so, Avril was a work in progress to Fabri. "She was so sheltered she didn't know blink-182 from Madonna," he continued. "She had no reference points because she was from a very religious family. Her mother kept pushing Faith Hill and Martina McBride at me, saying, 'This is Avril.'"

Fabri disagreed. With his help, Avril would soon discover her true musical self.

A New Direction

*F*abri wasted no time in trying to introduce Avril to music industry executives. He encouraged her to start writing her own songs and made a video of Avril singing onstage that he sent to several record labels. One of the people she met early on was Nettwerk Records vice president Mark Jowett.

Although he thought she had talent, he told MTV, "I don't know if she herself had a clear picture of her direction yet. I think her parents liked country quite a lot, and there was a part of her that was attracted to that kind of music."

Jowett agreed to produce a demo. Hoping to expand her musical horizons, he sent Avril to New York to work with some songwriters. Ken Krongard, a talent scout for Arista Records, happened to be in New

York in late 2000. He stopped by the studio where Avril was working and heard her perform. He was impressed enough to arrange for Avril to meet the head of the record label, famed producer Antonio "L.A." Reid.

"All I knew was that if I sang for this guy and if he liked me, that would make me able to get a record and that's all I wanted," she told Maeve Quigley of the *Sunday Mirror*. "Basically I wanted my CD."

She was about to get her wish. After just 15 minutes, Reid was convinced she could be a star. He offered Avril a deal that guaranteed her to be paid $1.25 million for two albums.

> **Famed record producer Antonio "L.A." Reid was convinced Avril could be a star.**

"I sang a couple of songs for him and he wanted to sign me right away," she would later tell Brian Pascual of Chartattack.com. "I wasn't even shopping for a deal! That doesn't happen very often. I mean, sometimes bands take 10 years to get a deal! So I was very, very, very lucky."

The most difficult part of this exciting turn of events was telling her parents she had decided to drop out of high school to pursue this opportunity.

"I wasn't going to turn it down—it's been my dream all my life," she said in the *Sunday Mirror* interview. Although her parents urged Avril to reconsider, her mind was made up. They eventually supported her decision. "They knew how much I wanted this and how much I've put into it," Avril explained.

Now that she had a record deal, Avril needed to come up with songs for the CD. It would prove to be a long and difficult process. She spent the next six months collaborating with a number of different songwriters. None of the songs worked. Even though she had been signed as a country singer, it really wasn't the kind of music she wanted to perform.

> *Once Avril had a record deal, coming up with songs for the CD became a long and difficult process.*

As Chris Willman of *Entertainment Weekly* observed, all these cowriters "failed to click with a girl who'd just discovered guitar-based rock and wasn't about to be kept down on the farm."

Avril later explained to Mary Dickie of the *Toronto Sun*, "I've always kind of been a fighter and stuck up for what I wanted. Everyone thought I'd be singing other people's songs and doing the pop thing, but I let them know very quickly that that's not what I wanted to do. I told them I wanted to write, and L.A. Reid told me to take my time and just figure it all out, so I did."

After Avril signed a record deal in 2000, she told her parents she was dropping out of high school to devote herself full time to recording her first CD. Although they initially argued for their daughter to finish her education first, they eventually supported Avril's decision.

Avril's breakthrough finally came when she flew to Los Angeles. She hooked up with the Matrix, a group of three songwriting/record producing partners: Lauren Christy, Graham Edwards and Scott Spock.

Christy told *Entertainment Weekly*, "She came to our studio and the record company was looking for Faith Hill-type songs, but she didn't seem to be into that at all. So we said, 'What do you want to do?' She said, 'I'm 16. I want to rock out.'"

Within a few hours, Avril and the Matrix wrote "Complicated." It would eventually be the first single from her debut album.

Over a few short months, Avril transformed herself and her music. She hired a new manager and adopted a new look: army fatigues, tank tops and long, straight hair that hung down in front of her face. Her new sound surprised a lot of people, including L.A. Reid, who admitted to *Entertainment Weekly*, "I was actually quite surprised to see the direction things took, because I thought it would be a little more...folky."

But as her new manager, Terry McBride, observed in the same *Entertainment Weekly* article, "When she was

> *Over a few months, Avril transformed herself and her music. She hired a new manager and adopted a new look.*

in Napanee she was true to what Napanee was. She was a product of that environment. But she's turned into a very worldly kid in a very short time period. You plop that girl in New York City — where there are 5,000 people in just one block — and you just put a kid in the candy store. Culture hit her over the head, and as with any teenager, it's like osmosis."

On her website, Avril agrees. "I'm just coming out and I'm going to clearly be myself — I write what I feel, I never worry what others think. I'm gonna dress what's me, I'm gonna act what's me and I'm gonna sing what's me."

In the process, Avril would become rock's newest sensation.

A More
Complicated Life

*A*vril's debut CD, *Let Go*, was released in the summer of 2002. On her website, she wrote, "So my CD is out now!!! It came out on the fourth. It was a special day for me. In a way it felt like my birthday. I'd like to thank everyone who purchased a copy. Your support is much appreciated!"

In the first months after the CD's release, Avril seemed tireless. Even though she never had a day off, she seemed to thrive on the excitement of watching her single climb the music charts. She wrote to her fans, "I can't wait to be out there; I want to rock the world! I want people to know that my music is real and honest—it came from my heart. I was just being true to myself."

From the beginning, Avril seemed determined not to be lumped in with other young female singers such as Britney Spears or Christina Aguilera. She adopted a tomboyish clothing style and steered clear of suggestive music videos that showed off her body. Avril didn't consider herself a pop diva—she was a rock singer, which is why her band is particularly important to her.

> **"I want people when they hear my name or think 'Avril Lavigne' to think of me and the guys," Avril explained to MTV.**

"I'm a solo artist and it's my name, but I have the band vibe and I want people, when they hear my name or think 'Avril Lavigne,' to think of me and the guys," she explained to MTV. "That's how much I want them to be involved in this. We have something really special and we connect really well. It's strange, but it really feels like we're all supposed to be together. It's a really cool, unique situation."

She wasn't worried about letting success go to her head. "It won't really make me change," she told ChartAttack.com. "I'm not worried about what other people say. I'm just going to be myself. I'm not going to try to pretend I'm someone else. I'm not a bad person. I like to have fun and I like to be myself. Hopefully, people will see that."

What they saw was a phenomenon. In February 2003, Avril was nominated for five Grammy awards, including best new artist, song of the year and best female pop performance for "Complicated," best pop vocal album for *Let Go*, and best female rock vocal performance for her second single, "Sk8er Boi."

"It's just the coolest thing to go home and be like, 'Yeah, mom and dad, I got nominated for a Grammy,'" Lavigne said during a CBS *Early Show* interview. "I

Avril has grown very close to the members of her band and goes out of her way to include them in her success. "We have something very special and we connect really well. It's a really cool, unique situation."

think that's so cool that we can say that for the rest of our lives."

Although Avril didn't win any Grammys, *Let Go* would become the highest selling North American CD of 2002. It eventually sold over six million copies worldwide and made Avril one of the music industry's brightest new stars.

> *Let Go would become the highest selling North American CD of 2002.*

She soon learned that there is a downside to being famous. In addition to a loss of privacy, there's a lot of hard work involved. After a year of non-stop touring and performing she told writer Mary Dickie, "I never get time off. Maybe after the tour I'll fly to the other side of the world so I can walk around without anyone saying anything to me."

She's had to deal with jealousy, even from people she grew up with. "I don't take it personally," she added to Dickie. "Some people are supportive, and others mock me and are rude. I guess it's weird for them 'cause they knew me at one point."

Avril also gets frustrated when people try to compare her to other singers. She tries to be philosophical.

"You just have to deal with it, especially if you're a new artist and people try and explain what you're like," she observed in her *Exclusive Magazine* interview. "I wouldn't compare myself to anyone. I have my own sound and my music is rock pop."

Avril knew it would be hard to duplicate the success of her first CD. But she is more interested in a long career than in breaking sales records, so she took her time recording her second CD, *Under My Skin*. She waited until May, 2004 to release it, making sure it was just right. "I'm a lot wiser now," she said to writer Joe D'Angelo of VH1.com. "Now I know what the business is like—what you have to do and how to work it. As a writer, I'm growing and my guitar-playing is getting better. I know what it's all about now, so I'm ready to go back out there and do it all again."

Avril is more interested in a long career than breaking sales records.

1984	Born on September 27 in Napanee, Ontario, Canada
1994	Enters Cornerstone Christian Academy
1996	Has role of Sally in *You're a Good Man Charlie Brown*
1998	Performs at the Quinte Spirit Festival
1999	Participates in first CD, *The Quinte Spirit*
1999	Is awarded the Robbie Lakins Award for Most Improved Graduate and the Marie Cowling Memorial Award for musical ability on graduation from Cornerstone
1999	Wins a radio contest and gets to sing a duet with Shania Twain
2000	Signs $1.25 million recording contract with Arista Records
2002	Releases first album, *Let Go*
2002	Wins *Best New Artist in a Video* at the *MTV Video Music* Awards
2003	Nominated for five Grammys
2003	Nominated for *Best Female Video* at the *MTV Video Music* Awards
2003	Wins two *Much Music Awards* for *Favorite Canadian Artist* and *Best International Video by a Canadian*
2004	Nominated for three Grammys
2004	Releases DVD *My World*
2004	Releases second album, *Under My Skin*

FOR FURTHER READING

D'Angelo, Joe. "Avril Lavigne Grows Up, Sheds Her Newbie Ways For Upcoming LP" VH1.com, November 6, 2003.

Kenyatta, Kelly. *Avril Lavigne: Anything but Ordinary*. Chicago: William H. Kelly, 2004.

Lavigne, Avril. *Let Go* (Piano/Vocal/Guitar). Milwaukee, Wisconsin: Hal Leonard, 2003.

Thorley, Joe. *Avril Lavigne: The Unofficial Book*. London: Virgin Publishing, 2003.

On the Internet
Official Website
www.avril-lavigne.com

MTV.com Bands
www.mtv.com/bands/az/lavigne_avril/artist.jhtml

Avril Lavigne Websites
www.avrilfans.com
www.alavigne.com
www.quintespirit.ca/avril.html
www.iq451.com/music/sites/avril-lavigne-web.htm

DISCOGRAPHY

INDEX